LEVEL UP NO MATTER WHAT

*7 Keys That Will Help Take
Your Life To New Heights*

Chuck Collins

Level Up No Matter What: 7 Keys That Will Help Take Your Life To New Heights

Chuck Collins
Copyright@ 2023
ISBN Paperback: 979-8-218-09970-1
ISBN Ebook: 979-8-218-10165-7
LCCN: 2022949276

For more inquiries, contact this email:
chuck@chuckcollinsbrand.com

Table of Contents

Foreword by Kenyatta Collins v

Introduction vii

Chuck's Life's Chronicles 1

Chuck's Key #1: Chase Your Dreams 11

Chuck's Key #2: Grow Your Mind 17

Chuck's Key #3: Share Your Gifts With the World......24

Chuck's Key #4: Find Friends That Motivate You 29

Chuck's Key #5: Take Care of Your Body 34

Chuck's Key #6: Be Grateful and Thankful
For It All 40

Chuck's Key #7: Bless Somebody Else 45

Conclusion 51

Foreword

In life situations have the tendency to become 'too difficult' or seem impossible to accomplish and many simply give up. They'd rather throw their hands up and walk away than to push themselves to their next level in life. On the other hand, many people just need a plan of action to get to that next level. If you have ever been on either end of this spectrum then get ready to be transformed!

Transformation occurs when you open your mind beyond what is in front of you to see a world of endless possibilities. This book is packed full of information geared to take you on a journey of self-discovery; and bring you back ready to hit the pavement running to get all that life has in store for you. The topics discussed within these pages can be used by all age groups regardless of race, gender, or culture. The only thing is that you have to be willing to apply them to your life every day. The blueprint has already been laid out for you in *Level Up No Matter What: 7 Keys That Will Help Take Your Life To New Heights*. What you choose to do is up to you.

My husband, author Chuck Collins can best be described in one word as tenacious. This is because of his grit, determination and persistence even in the face of adversity. He is no stranger to life's ups and downs but the difference is his ability to press forward in times of uncertainty. Over the years Chuck has learned the power of positive affirmations and the strength of one's mindset. From that he developed 7 Keys that are designed to help get you to your next level of greatness.

Having known Chuck for over 27 years and married to him for 9 of them, I can say without a shadow of a doubt that he is a visionary, a leader, a mentor to many, a mindset coach, and a business coach. He has the gift to ignite any room when he speaks and he strives to promote positivity and growth in others. *Level Up No Matter What: 7 Keys That Will Help Take Your Life To New Heights* was a labor of love. A publication that you will want to read again and again; with new eye-opening perspectives each time. So what are you waiting for? Let's Level Up!!

Kenyatta Collins MSN, RN, FNP-C
CEO, Affinity Private Home Care Inc
Certified Life Coach

Introduction

Congratulations! If you have decided to read this book, you are at least curious about taking your life to the next level, no matter what it takes. By picking up this book, you are already one step closer to learning about the keys that will unlock your potential and improve your life.

What's the next level? We all want to know, right? But the honest answer to that question is this: THE HARD PART because designing the blueprint for the rest of your life begins now.

If you are anything like me, my parents or my support system handled most of the tough decisions during my youth. I just followed their lead without any input. During those times, it was almost like I was watching a 3D movie without those special 3D glasses. But do you know what happens if you're in one of those 3D movies without the glasses? Yep, you're right. It is extremely blurry, and the picture is distorted.

My life was blurry. However, as soon as I graduated from high school, I began to regain sight of my life. And boy, it was coming at me fast! It was like someone had just handed me a pair of those special glasses, and I started to see life for what it really was.

I felt like I was in the fast lane during those times. I was experiencing things for the first time like:

- *Debt*
- *Stress*
- *Family Issues*
- *New Relationships*
- *Loss of Relationships*

In my experience, losing relationships is real, especially when you are striving to go to a higher level in your life. Whether your next level is to attend a college or university, military service, landing a job in corporate America, entrepreneurship, or job promotions, please understand and be ready to lose some relationships. When you are determined to get the most out of life, you will discover that it is a tough and lonely road that is not meant for everyone. You will not be able to take everyone with you as you achieve higher goals.

People will start to notice something different about you. It may even surprise you about who will last in your life and who will not last in your life, which may lead to you having haters. But a wise man once said, *"If you ain't got no haters, you ain't popping."*

I am sure you are definitely popping. So, get ready to have some haters in your life. Chances are you are thinking of about three haters in your head at this very moment.

Here is my challenge for you. It's quite simple. I challenge you to get to the next level no matter what. I repeat, get to the next level no matter what. That next level will be different for everybody who accepts the challenge. But no matter where you are in life or whatever you are going through, you should always strive to take your life to higher heights.

Your time on this earth is limited. So please don't waste it worrying about haters or living someone else's life. We all have the right and the responsibility to design our own lives and create our own paths. I have written this book to encourage and challenge you to get to that next level.

Let's get one thing straight—I'm not here trying to sell you a pipe dream. I am not here to tell you that by listening to me, what comes next in your life will be easy. I cannot and will not do that.

In fact, you should know that your life will never be easy. Lord knows I haven't had an easy life. Honestly, I thank God that I don't look like what I've been through. Nevertheless, I have learned to put in the work to go to the next level no matter what. My purpose in writing this book is to share my story and keys to next-level living as a step-by-step guide for you as you embark on your next-level journey.

Chuck's Life's Chronicles

My life has been one interesting rollercoaster. Full of ups, downs, highs, and lows. I was born and raised in Louisville, Kentucky. Most people only know Louisville, Kentucky, for two reasons. The first reason is because of the Kentucky Derby. The other reason is Muhammad Ali. And now you know three reasons. I'm from there.

While growing up in Louisville, like many of you, I had to deal with some traumatic experiences early in life. My first traumatic experience was when my older cousin was murdered the day before my ninth birthday, down the street from my house. Like most nine-year-olds, I had no worries. That was until this tragedy shook my family to the core back in the spring of May 1992.

I grew up with a great family. We were a tight-knit group. We were always around each other. I mean, how could we not be? I could visit most of my relatives in just a short five-minute walk.

My aunt and uncle owned a home on one side of the street. Directly across the street from them was my grandparents' home. Then on my side of the street, we just happened to live across the street from another aunt and uncle and their home. As a kid, I had it so good that if I didn't like what my mom cooked for dinner, I could call around to my family to see what they had to determine if they had a better option and if they did, I was there.

As the days got closer to my ninth birthday, life was good. As usual, my family was in good spirits, this time because my older cousin from across the street had just turned 21. Up next was my birthday in just a few days, and I was pumped. But little did I know how much my life would change before my birthday arrived.

A week after celebrating his 21st birthday, and the day before my birthday, my cousin was killed in a drive-by shooting. Being so young at the time, I don't remember the details of my cousin's murder. But I remember that after May 27, 1992, our family was no longer the same. Our family was forever changed in the early hours of May 27, 1992. My cousin's murder stole our joy, and we could never get it back as a family.

My Sister Is Pregnant?

Another traumatic experience was when my then-teenage sister found out she was pregnant at the age of fifteen. My sister and I have this running debate on which of us is our parents' favorite child. Back in the day, there was no question about it. My sister was the golden child. During my elementary years and much of my middle school days, I was the rebel in the family. I remember many days when I would come home from school with terrible grades and hear, "Why can't you be more like your sister?"

It's not like I wasn't trying to be like my sister. My sister is three years older than me. In my eyes, she was one of the cool kids. She was the one who had to teach her little brother how to dress, dance, and be cool. She even introduced me to rap music. As I said, she was the golden child. But as my sister entered high school, her grip on being the golden child started to loosen.

One day after school, as I was walking home from the bus stop, I noticed that my mom and sister were really emotional. After my mom stormed off to go inside the house, I asked my sister what had happened. My sister wiped her tears away and told me she was pregnant. She was fifteen.

That day will never leave my memory because it was the day that my childhood ended. I became a young adult at the age of twelve. My relationship changed with my mom, my dad, and my sister. At twelve, I often felt emotionally alone and abandoned by the people I needed the most. For the next few years, our home turned cold. What used to be a home full of love, laughter, and togetherness turned into a house full of shame, embarrassment, depression, and bitterness.

Realizing what my sister's teenage pregnancy did to my family, I understood just how important it was for me to take care of myself, oftentimes by myself. So in the midst of the family drama, somehow, I was able to focus on school and turn myself into a scholar.

Robbed At Gunpoint

Also, let's not forget about the time at the age of twenty when I was robbed at gunpoint while working a shift at the local drug store. It's crazy how your life can change in the blink of an eye, but this is exactly what happened to me at the age of twenty. What started as a somewhat normal weekend almost came to a tragic ending for me. In less than 24 hours, I went from living my best life with friends at a party to staring down the barrel of a loaded gun.

Like most college kids at the time, I had a part-time job that I worked on the weekends when I didn't have too much going on with school. I worked at a local drug store located directly in the middle of the "hood." But I never had too many issues, so I didn't feel unsafe.

On this particular weekend, I was scheduled to work the morning shift. I was always happy to work the morning shift on the weekends because it allowed me to go out with my friends, wake up, go to work, and get back to school at a decent time. This weekend was no exception. My plan was to attend a party with my friends, then wake up early and get to work.

As usual, the party was so much fun. Me and my boys cut up with one another, danced, and enjoyed ourselves the whole time. I even saw a female coworker at the party. She and I were on the schedule to work the following day. As the party ended, I hopped into my car and went straight home.

The next morning I woke up and headed to work just like any other day. But almost as soon as I arrived at the store, I realized this would not be an ordinary day.

After I clocked in for my shift, I settled into my workstation until 8 am. After that, I headed to unlock the automatic doors at the front of the store. While completing my tasks, I talked to my coworker about the party we had both attended. Then the unthinkable happened.

Suddenly, a man in a ski mask appeared with his gun out in front of him. As the gunman approached, my female coworker hit the floor and started crying loudly. I froze. Then the gunman grabbed me. He shoved the gun to my head while demanding all of the money from the register.

He was loud and aggressive. It all seemed like a movie. I moved as fast as I could to open the cash register. As I opened the register, I noticed my coworker was still lying on the ground, crying.

She was loud. The gunman was getting even louder. This entire scene had me tripping. I knew things were going to escalate when I had to inform him that there was no money in the register because the store had just opened. And just like in the movies, my life flashed before my eyes. I had a funny feeling that this entire situation would not end well. Honestly, I felt as though I was about to die.

"Get off the ground," the gunman screamed at my female coworker. He ordered us to lead him to the store's safe. Our journey towards the safe was interrupted by a blaring car

horn. I later found out that this was the gunman's accomplice signaling him that it was time to leave before the police arrived. The events after the horn are blurry details. However, I remember that the gunman left the store without harming my coworkers or me.

Leveling Up After Graduating College

As I said, my life has been interesting. Despite all of the trauma, I have always been driven to go to higher heights in life. Remaining complacent was never a goal of mine. Next-level living was a constant desire for me.

For example, as a pre-teen, my mom had stopped footing the bill for my teenage outings. So, I started my lawn care service to make money. This forced me to devise a master plan.

Every two weeks or so, my good buddy and I would pack up our borrowed lawnmowers, a rake, a mask, and a can of gas and find paying clients. Instead of being down because my mother refused to support my social life, I leveled up to become an entrepreneur. This was the first time I implemented my "level-up no matter what" philosophy.

After graduating from college, I was ready to level up and relocate with one of my good friends. Atlanta, Georgia, was our destination of choice. Everything was planned and was running smoothly. This should have been a high moment but quickly turned into a low moment when my buddy changed his mind.

I was crushed. Nevertheless, I followed through with my relocation plans. Often, no matter how much you want family and friends to join you, going to new heights will require you to launch into new endeavors alone. However, my journey to Atlanta would become a solo journey. This was a level-up learning experience.

Leveling Up The Corporate Ladder

Life in Atlanta continued to take me to many different heights. For years, I scurried my way up the corporate ladder. But much like being on an airplane, there will be unexpected turbulence at some levels. My corporate success became shaky.

Another opportunity presented itself for which I had to take a leap of faith and leave my position to accept the job at another company. But do you remember the character Craig from the hit movie starring Ice Cube and Chris Tucker named *Friday*? Do you remember how Craig got fired on his day off? That was what happened to me.

Right after I resigned from my job, a few days before my new job was set to begin, I received an email saying that there was no job to come to. The company that gave me the new job decided to rescind their job offer.

I can still remember it like it was yesterday. When we received this email, my wife Kenyatta and I were in Puerto Rico, waiting in a Wendy's drive-thru in the pouring rain. Crushed again, I couldn't help but think to myself, "Wow, Chuck, how did you get fired before you even started?" It was one of the lowest moments of my life.

Yet, little did I know that this was another level up, no matter what moment in action. I could either sulk over this disappointment or stand up in it and devise another master plan. I chose to stand up.

In my hot garage in my home in Atlanta, in the middle of July, with just an idea and my computer, I started my first company as an adult. I was determined to level up professionally no matter what my circumstances resembled. Upon returning from Puerto Rico, I duplicated the adrenaline I had when my mom told me that she was no longer giving me money for my social outings.

In the movies, this is the part where I was supposed to ride off in the sunset and become super rich and famous. Well, that's not how my story went. For a while, I sucked at being an entrepreneur. I can't even lie. I made tons of mistakes.

This new level was difficult for me. I almost quit a bunch of times. I got depressed. I got scared. I got lonely even though I had a wife and a daughter under my roof.

Not reaching the goals you set for yourself will usher in insecurity. I questioned myself constantly. This entrepreneurial experience was beating me up like the boxer Mike Tyson did his opponents. But I refused to quit. I kept going. Like the young people say, *"I had to get this thing out of the mud."*

Partnering with like-minded people helps you to level up no matter what. Eventually, I started to find my footing. I began to network and meet some great people who would later become my business partners. They understood what I meant when I told them I wanted to go to the next level.

I started to make a few deals. I even heard my wife bragging about me one day while she was talking to someone on the phone. You talk about a confidence booster. It was a great feeling to hear my life partner share her happiness with others about how I was making strides in my newfound company.

There were other challenging times. I swear, I could write a different book about some of the things my family and I endured while leveling up, no matter what. But who knew that my greatest mess would also become my greatest message?

I overcame many hardships and pain in order to take my life to new heights. Things such as cancer infecting my mother's body. My wife was involved in a devastating car accident that could have easily killed her. To add gasoline to the fire, an illness attacked my daughter, causing her to lose feeling in most of her limbs temporarily. There were countless other hurdles that had me tossing and turning. Still, I remained steadfast and unmovable because I was ready to level up.

Remember this critical fact; life isn't fair. Life is life. But know it will be worth it whenever you chase your dreams and continue to push through in the end.

You should be confident that whatever you want out of this life, you can obtain it. And why should you be confident? Let me take you to a scripture in the Bible.

"Now this is the confidence that we have in Him, that if we ask anything according to His will, He hears us. And if we know that he hears us, whatever we ask, we know that we have the petitions that we have asked of Him," (1 John 5:14-15).

The Bible says that life will smack you down whenever you try your hardest to get to that next level. However, you must remain confident that God has your back. You should have the faith to believe that God will provide you with whatever you desire. This will happen, but only after you are tested repeatedly.

Again, going to the next level will take a lot of work. However, this book will guide you to keep moving to manifest your next level. I have given you my 7 keys to next-level success. I call them *"Chuck's Keys."*

But let me warn you. If you use these 7 keys, you better get ready to experience tangible results. Using my keys will usher you to new heights that you never knew existed. Are you really ready to level up no matter what?

Chuck's Key #1:

Chase Your Dreams

I have been a big-time dreamer for as long as I can remember. When I was a kid, I had a wild imagination. So much so that I believed that I could grow to 6 foot 6 and play in the NBA just like my favorite basketball player Sir Charles Barkley. So I went to my mom and let her know that pretty soon she wouldn't have to work anymore because I was going to be rich, and I would take care of her.

She then asked me how I was going to take care of her. I told her about my big plan. I'm going to grow to 6 foot 6 and play in the NBA. She looked me straight in the eye and told me I could be anything I wanted to be as long as I was willing to work hard for it. Then she walked out of the room as fast as she could.

As an adult, I know exactly why she walked out of the room so fast. It was to laugh a little because she knew in her heart that this dream would be hard to achieve. Not only making it to the NBA but definitely the whole 6-foot-6 thing.

The problem with this dream was that my mom stood 5 feet, and my dad was no taller than 5 foot 10. Eventually, after all of my friends began to tower over me and after I was cut from the high school varsity my sophomore and junior years, I realized that I might need to find a different dream to chase.

Pretty soon, I came up with another dream. Then another dream. Then another dream. The problem was I only sometimes chased after them. They only remained dreams. But if you want everything life has to offer, you must chase your dreams.

Chasing your dreams is the most important thing in the world. But it is only for those who dare to take a chance to believe. It requires hope, courage, deep inspiration, and total commitment. We can all chase our dreams, but most choose not to.

Why? As I stated earlier, chasing your dreams requires courage and complete determination, especially if the results take longer than we all want them to. When you are serious about your goals, be ready to be alone, laughed at, doubted, criticized, and misunderstood.

Back when it was just me, my computer, and my ideas in that hot garage, I can assure you that I didn't have much money, knowledge, or even the right resources. But I had a positive attitude, patience, and persistence. Les Brown, the legendary motivational speaker, says a positive attitude combined with patience and persistence will help carry you through when chasing your dreams begins to get harder and harder.

But as they say, anything worth doing is going to be hard. And even in the hard times, chasing your dreams makes life worth living. It will give your life purpose and meaning because a man with a vision and a little bit of faith is unstoppable.

The Importance of a Positive Attitude

Chasing your dreams can be a humbling experience. For me, it most definitely was. Remember, my dreams began inside a hot garage in July. When I was in the garage making phone calls and trying to strike up business with prospects, I always tried to smile as much as possible.

I found out that having a positive attitude made me happy while I was on the phone. Why? It was a mind trick for me. In my mind, smiling reminded me that I needed a positive attitude while chasing my dreams. Even if I were uncomfortable in the moment, I felt that if my attitude remained positive, I could enjoy the process better.

Being happy on the phone increased my productivity at work. Being more productive at work led to more business leads. More business leads led to more appointments. More appointments led to more offers. More offers led to more money.

The Importance of Patience

We all know that dreams can seem hard to achieve sometimes. But most of us also think that we will be the ones who have instant success in whatever dream we are chasing. That was me. I just knew that on my first few business deals, I would strike it rich, and it would be all good for the rest of my life from that point on.

Well, that was not the case for me. What I found out is that my dream was going to cost me more time and money than I thought. Because truthfully, I was not a particularly good businessman at first. I was nervous, anxious, and in above my head during those early days of running my company. Sometimes I was downright terrible on the phone.

What I found out quickly was that chasing my dream was going to take more time than I had imagined. As the saying goes, good things come to those who wait. This is why it is so important to remain patient with yourself.

According to Kira Newman of Greater Good Magazine, *"the road to achievement is a long one, and we must have the patience to wait calmly in the face of frustration or adversity."* Of course, I wanted to be a successful businessman right away. However, when that did not happen, I knew the best thing for me would be to develop patience for myself and my journey. By developing patience for myself, I was able to reduce stress. Developing patience also gave me the time to grow the skills that I needed to master to become a better businessman.

The Importance of Persistence

Chasing your dreams will require you to develop persistence. Persistence will help pick you up for the 10th time after you have fallen for the 9th time. By developing persistence, you can push through challenges and failures.

I needed persistence during the early days of chasing my dreams. On those days when it seemed like no progress was being made or when my bank account would get lower and lower and nothing seemed to go my way, persistence kept me going.

Persistence can be a superpower. It is for my daughter. Whenever she has her mind set on something, she will keep asking me or her mom about it until she gets her way. I know for a fact that persistence has earned her a bike, computer, tablet, new shoes, new clothes, and an apple watch.

Being persistent allowed me to keep showing up daily in the hot garage for my dreams. Persistence allowed me not to give up when no one was calling me back. Persistence allowed me to make one more phone call when I had just got told no on the previous call. And eventually, persistence got me my first business deal.

Persistence did not allow me to abandon my dreams. Persistence allowed me to chase my dreams without holding back, pushing me out of my comfort zone. And once I was outside my comfort zone, I realized I could achieve anything in this lifetime.

Be The Best To Ever Do It

What dream are you chasing? What do you wish to become, a doctor, lawyer, nurse, engineer, mom, dad, or teacher? Whatever you choose to be, be sure to chase your dreams to become the best to ever do it. The dream I had was to become a successful businessman.

When I started my first company in my garage, I started with the goal of earning 15 million dollars one day. Later I changed that goal to earn $100 million dollars or more in my lifetime. Even then, I had every intention of becoming one of the best businessmen ever. I wanted to create a business I could eventually pass down to my kids and grandkids. I wanted to be so good at a business that people would come from far and wide to work with me.

I am still a work in progress, but my goal is to finish what I started and strive to be the best. Your goal should be similar.

Chuck's Key #2:

Grow Your Mind

Growing your mind is the hardest of the 7 keys you will ever have to master. In order to get to the next level, you have to change the way you think. The mind is constantly in motion like a revolving door. It is up to you to determine what is allowed inside the door and what is not. And to grow your mind, your thoughts must be thoroughly analyzed.

To get to the next level in life, you must change how you use the mind and its power. The mind manages each person's imagination, consciousness, thinking, judgments, intelligence, perception, and memory. It even controls your instincts and emotions.

The mind, without a doubt, is the most powerful and essential element each person possesses. It can control the whole of a person's life, which can be good or bad, depending on how each person grows their mind. However, the mind is not easy to control or grow. It can't be controlled just because we wish it without acting on it. For the mind to grow, it must be constantly attended to.

The mind will need to be fed. What you feed your mind becomes your reality. The way to grow the mind is to feed it with as much positive information as possible. The ideas and thoughts you allow to enter your mind make you the person you will become.

How to Grow Your Mind

To get to the next level, we must know how to grow and control our minds in a positive manner. The mind can be led in both right and wrong ways, depending on what the person involved chooses. But if we want to make a difference, our minds should remain focused on the positive.

Thinking negatively is relatively easy. Yet, changing your mindset is extremely hard to master. Again, the mind is not easy to control. It will not grow if you don't feed it correctly. Below are the steps I recommend to help you grow your mind.

Read Your Bible

I'm sure you may be rolling your eyes at me because I am telling you to "read your Bible." Trust me. I get it. When I was younger, it would immediately turn me off whenever someone suggested I read the Bible to find an answer. But if you bear with me for a little bit, I will explain.

When I say, "read your Bible," I am not suggesting that you grab the Bible off the top of your bookcase, blow the dust off the cover, and start reading nonstop from page 1 to page 5000 (I don't know how many pages are in the Bible). I suggest you read the Bible enough to learn some scriptures and verses you can remember.

Trust me, this will come in handy when nothing makes sense in the natural world, and you need to reach the supernatural world for help. Reading the Bible teaches you how to have enough faith to pray instead of worrying. The Bible gives you strength, understanding, and advice. It will give your life clarity by explaining the supernatural favor of God over your life.

Here are some of my favorite Bible scriptures you can start with:

- *Faith is the substance of things hoped for and the evidence of things not seen.* - Hebrews 11:1

- *You have not because you ask not.* - James 4:2

- *Write the vision; make it plain.* - Habakkuk 2:2

Start from scratch. Learn how to read the Bible for understanding. Then you will realize how helpful it can be to grow your mind.

Read Inspirational Books

Sounds simple enough, right? Read books that inspire you to want more out of life. Read books that make you think and feel differently. Read books that will change your views about life. Books that cause you to make immediate changes away from past choices that may have resulted from fear and hurt you've once taught yourself.

One of the best books I recently read was Kevin Hart's *"I Can't Make This Up."* I'm not just saying that because we are the same size, but because of the obstacles that he had to overcome in his lifetime to get to where he is now. His story was truly inspirational. Reading his book made me think and feel differently. By reading his chapters, I was led to believe that I, too, could reach the next level in life by changing the way I thought.

I also recommend the following books:

- *The Success Principles* by Jack Canfield

- *Think and Grow Rich A Black Choice* by Dennis Kimbro and Napoleon Hill

- *The Magic of Thinking Big* by David J. Schwartz

These books challenged me to change my thinking to create a better life. Check those books out for yourself. Who knows? These books will be inspirational for you and your journey also.

Use Positive Affirmations

My other suggestion to help grow your mind is to practice using positive affirmations. You can determine your destiny with the words that you speak. So, you should practice the use of positive affirmations daily. You should make it an everyday routine to speak positivity into your lives regardless of the situation you may find yourself in.

Believe me, these affirmations help in critical situations. It can be weird when you first start to do these positive affirmations. So to make it less weird, let's practice doing some affirmations together.

Here are a few examples of positive affirmations that I use each day. I have these posted in my closet and read them aloud before bedtime. Let's say these together:

- *I am the best*
- *I can do it*
- *God is always with me*
- *I am a winner*
- *Today is my day*

Repeat it again
- *I am the best*
- *I can do it*
- *God is always with me*
- *I am a winner*
- *Today is my day*

Here are a few examples of some powerful business affirmations. Me and my wife Kenyatta have these posted in our home office. We recite these each day before we do any work. If you have a business, let's say these together:

- *I am a success magnet.*

- *My business is a huge success.*

- *I am a champion. I am the best at what I do.*

- *I have created the perfect business for myself.*

- *I attract the ideal clients for my business.*

- *Success and prosperity effortlessly flow to me.*

- *I am worthy of great success in my business.*

- *My work makes a positive difference in this world.*

- *My business income is growing faster than I ever imagined.*

- *I have everything I need within me to be wildly successful in business.*

- *I am thankful for everyone who has contributed to my business success–my team and my clients.*

The easiest way to remember to recite the positive affirmations is to place them on your bathroom mirror. That way, you can read them out loud when you brush your teeth in the morning and before bed. Once you begin to use these affirmations, be sure to take a moment to visualize yourself as what you are reciting.

You can also listen to positive affirmations while you sleep. This is what I do. Each night before I fall asleep, I plug my phone into the charger and find a 2-hour affirmation channel on YouTube, Amazon Music, Spotify, or Apple music to play. That way, my brain can absorb the positivity while it rests, and I will wake up refreshed and ready to act on the positive thoughts from the previous night.

Use Vision Boards

I once read that a man with a dream and a little bit of faith is an unstoppable man. Vision boards help you keep track of your dreams while also giving you the faith that they will eventually become a reality if you keep working towards them. That's what vision boards can do for you. I have a vision board in my closet that I look at each night at 10 pm.

Many items on my vision board have become a reality, like my dream house and becoming an author. There are things like my dream car, dream house, dream physique, and bank account balance on my vision board. I recently test-drove my dream car, so it's only a matter of time before I mark that one off of the list too. On the other hand, I still have room for improvement, like speaking fluent Spanish.

However, I am on the right track, and with the help of my vision board, I will be able to speak fluent Spanish the next time I go to Cancun. Let's just say uno momento for now! Make sure to put it in plain sight when you set up your vision board. Creating a great vision board that you will never see will do you no good. What would you put on your vision board?

Chuck's Key #3:

Share Your Gifts With the World

There are certain things that God specifically has for you and only you. God gives each of us a unique gift that no one else has. Using your gifts leads to faster growth and development. When you tap into these gifts, your potential becomes limitless. Share your gifts with the world and watch what happens.

God gave us a gift the moment we were formed in our mother's womb. This gift defines everyone; it distinguishes us from one another and makes us unique. Your gift is the special attribute of yours that relates you with Him. Once you find your gift, you must use it wisely, or it can be taken away.

What is Your Gift?

What is your gift? What gifts do you have inside of you that could make the world a better place? Who knows, maybe you have the cure for cancer? Perhaps you have the singing voice of an angel? No matter what gifts you possess, the world is waiting for you to share them.

You will know when you have found your gift because it will be easy for you but amazing to the world. In other words, your gift will be the thing you can do best with the least amount of effort. No matter how big or small, everyone has their own gift, but it is up to you to recognize it.

For the longest time, I used to believe that my gift was only in entrepreneurship. I thought my gift was to create successful businesses for my family and me, but this changed a few years ago.

In 2019, I was invited to be the keynote speaker for a community scholarship foundation in my hometown of Louisville, Kentucky. Although I was extremely nervous about speaking because most of my friends and family would be in attendance, I accepted the invitation to be the keynote speaker and attended the event.

As I was giving the speech, I felt something in my spirit change. It felt like there was an awakening happening inside of me. I felt like I belonged on the stage, giving the audience some motivational advice. I executed my speech beautifully enough that I got a standing ovation.

At that very moment, as I walked off that stage, I realized that I had just operated in my gift. Since that day, I have worked towards my motivational speaker gift. That 2019 speech ended up being the catalyst for this book.

The Best Way to Use Your Gifts

The best way to utilize God's gifts is to share them. Why is it so important to share your gifts? Well, because the process of sharing your gifts will serve to open your world in ways you can't even imagine. Sharing your gifts with the world will provide you a way to give back to the universe, not because you have to but because it allows others to learn, grow and advance in ways they have yet to experience.

Steve Harvey did a great job explaining this theory in his speech *Follow Your Gift, Not Your Passion*. Steve explained in a very comical way that people waste so much time and money chasing fortune and fame in every way they can think of while disregarding the easiest way, which is using our gifts.

Steve Harvey has become an expert in following his gift. In his speech, he said we should stop running away from our gifts and stop trying to be something at which we are not gifted. By using our gifts, we can not only change ourselves, but we can also change the world.

Today, Steve Harvey is a movie star, TV star, radio star, and author. By using his gift of comedy, Steve has been able to become a media mogul. Steve is also a well-respected motivational speaker who uses his story to change the lives of his audiences.

Live By Purpose

Sharing your gift with others will not take away from what you have but will add to your life. Your life will improve when you share your gift with someone else. Sharing your gift will also help clarify your purpose in life. Who you are and what you are meant to do with your life are all defined by your life's purpose.

There is a direct connection between finding your purpose and reaching your potential. You will never fulfill your destiny doing work that you hate. Many greats have spoken on the importance of the day they found their life's purpose. Seeing their life's purpose has taken many people to the next level because they found that when you work for your purpose, your purpose will begin to work for you.

When you align your gift with your purpose, you set yourself up for a great life. When you find your purpose, use your purpose to make the world better. Your purpose will not be about money or fame but how you serve the people around you. Keep your purpose your priority because it will make you great. Your greatness will be defined by how much your life makes a difference, even in the slightest way. Make greatness your new norm.

Muhammad Ali

When it comes to greatness, a few people come to mind. But by me being a product of Louisville, Kentucky, it didn't take me that long to think about Muhammed Ali. Like many others, I regard Muhammad Ali as my hero. He is also a prime example of how sharing your gifts can change the world.

Who knew a young, bad, ghetto kid with a clever mind named Cassius Clay could accomplish so much? Ali did. He believed in himself so much that he knew he was the greatest before the rest of the world caught on. He understood who he was. Ali knew where he came from and where he was going. Using grit, determination, and sacrifice, he dedicated his life to sharing his gifts with the world.

Those gifts allowed him to become a champion of the boxing ring and a champion of the people. Sure he is the most famous boxer to have ever lived, at least in my eyes. He was the world boxing champion on three occasions. More importantly, later in his life, he used his gifts as a humanitarian to challenge the world to change.

Ali knew his purpose and walked in his truth. This allowed him to elevate to a level of greatness that few other people have been able to achieve. Because Muhammad Ali chose to share his gifts with the world, he is revered globally. All in all, God wants us to share our gifts for the betterment of ourselves and the world. Sharing your gift is one of the things that makes God happy, and He blesses abundantly for it.

Chuck's Key #4:

Find Friends That Motivate You

As you embark on your journey to the next level, you will meet all sorts of people. Some people will be in your life for a reason, while others will only be in your life for a season. There will be people who are connectors and others who are just associates. But with all of the people that you meet, only a few of these people will be able to be called friends.

The people you call friends should be reserved for the positive people who believe in your dreams, encourage your ideas, support your ambitions, and bring out the best in you. You will recognize these friends when you meet them because they will be the ones who talk about plans, goals, and aspirations but never seem to have the time to talk about the people that they don't like.

These types of people never seem to have the time to talk about unnecessary things. They will be the ones that force you to step your game up. Remember those haters we spoke of earlier in the book? Remember this, too. You can't do epic things with basic people. Find friends that motivate you.

Who Are Your Friends?

Who are your friends? Look around yourself. Take a good look at your friends and be honest. Are you motivated by your current friends? Being friends with the wrong people has been disastrous for many people. A famous quote reads, "If you show me your friends, I'll show you your future."

In one of his speeches, the great Denzel Washington stated that if you hang around five confident people, you will be the 6th. If you hang around five intelligent people, you will be the 6th. If you hang around five millionaires, you will be the 6th.

Similarly, if you hang around five idiots, you will be the 6th. If you hang around five hopeless people, you will become the 6th. If you hang around five haters, you will become the 6th. So again, who are your friends?

Find friends who will uplift you. Surround yourself with confidants who bring out the best in you. If you realize that you have been hanging out with friends that are not good for your life, there is still time to leave them. If you're truly ready to embark on the journey to the next level, find positive friends that will force you to level up with them. Become friends with people who have achieved a lot in life and abandon the negative friends you have.

Friends contribute significantly to your life, so it is crucial to choose the right friends, especially when you're aiming for greater heights in life. Wilfred Peterson says we should strive to walk with dreamers, believers, courageous, cheerful planners, doers, the successful people with their heads in the clouds and feet on the ground. These friends will impact our lives positively if we associate with them.

Too often, we don't realize who we are. As a result, we allow negative voices to convince us that we are limited. Remember, the people you spend most of your time with are whom you will eventually mirror, so you must surround yourself with people that will make you want more in life, not those that will bring you down with their talks and negative thoughts.

Aim to befriend goal achievers, goal chasers, hard workers, and motivators who won't hesitate to pull you through when you make a mistake in life. Surround yourself with people who have conquered the mission you are about to start. It would be best if you associated with people who inspire you every second, every day.

Find people who will challenge you to rise higher and want more in life, who make you better than you already are. Don't waste your valuable time with people that are not adding to your growth. When you hang with people who cannot add to your life, you also will see that life won't progress. Your destiny is too important for that.

Quality Over Quantity

Nowadays, we live in a Facebook, Instagram, and TikTok world, and people enjoy having as many friends as they possibly can. Another thing you should be mindful of when trying to find these friends is the quantity. But I'm telling you now that if you want to get to the next level, focus less on the quantity and more on the quality of your friends.

Your friends should motivate and inspire you, and your circle should be well-rounded and supportive. The larger the circle, the harder it will be to keep the energy high. So keep your friends as tight as possible. It can be disastrous to have a large number of friends. You only need to ensure that the people you choose as your friends will elevate your life, even if there are only a few. If you cannot change the people around you, you must change the people around you.

Lebron James

Lebron James is one of the best examples of someone who has mastered the quality over quantity method when choosing friends. The business of Lebron James is booming. A lot of his fortune was made by being a once-in-a-generation type of professional basketball player.

Whenever Lebron decides to retire from the NBA, he will go down as one of the greatest basketball players of all time. However, outside of the basketball court, Lebron James has built a global empire by strategically tapping into the quality of his three friends. Lebron could have chosen anyone to help him with his success off the court. Instead, he has empowered one of his friends, Maverick Carter, to be his business manager.

His friend Rich Paul is his sports agent. His friend Randy Mims is his chief of staff, who travels with Lebron and manages his day-to-day operations. Recently, it was announced that Lebron James is officially a billionaire. That is Billionaire with a B. So they must be doing something right over there at Lebron James Inc!! It's wise to say that Lebron understands the importance of the quality of your friends.

Now while I don't have the privilege of being a billionaire like Lebron (yet), I do share in his philosophy of surrounding myself with only a small circle. I know that I can't share my vision with people who are blind, so in my inner circle, you will find all stand-up individuals who are dedicated to holding each one of us accountable.

We are an eclectic group. From youth ministers to accountants. From gospel music legend Kirk Franklin to gangster rappers such as Lil Baby. I may not see my friends for days, weeks, or even months, but our bond is always there. Who knows what moves we may make in the future? My friends may one day make me a billionaire. Only time will tell. But my friends motivate me to dig deep and challenge myself to reach newer levels. How about your friends?

Chuck's Key #5:

Take Care of Your Body

You have only one body. You have to take care of it. As you know, I am not a doctor, health coach, or a personal trainer. But as an entrepreneur, it takes a lot of physical and mental effort to get to the next level. To maintain that level of physical and mental effort, you must take care of your body.

Take care of your body. I repeat, take care of your body. Try to keep it simple, watch what you eat, watch what you drink, and exercise whenever you can. You're not going to be this age for long, so remember your health is your greatest wealth.

Health issues, even the smallest ones, can interfere with and may even overshadow your life plans. Poor health can increase stress and produce unfavorable sicknesses in the body. And not only that, but poor health can also create challenges that will jeopardize your way of living.

Your health is the most vital key listed in this book because it helps balance you physically and mentally. It makes zero sense to achieve your goals finally, become a success, make money, and then give it all away to the hospital with bad health. So in this section, we will go briefly into how to take care of our bodies properly to avoid unhealthy situations.

Take Care Of Your Body

I understand how hard it is to take care of your body. I love hamburgers, pizza, candy, soda, French fries, and lemon pepper mild wings like the next man. But at some point, these foods started not to love me back. At one point, fast food was breakfast, lunch, and dinner and my body started to show it. I was five foot nothing and almost two hundred pounds. Something had to change.

Think about this. Chasing your dreams is hard if you're always out of breath. When it comes to taking care of your body, try to keep a consistent routine and keep it simple. Taking care of your body requires you to be mindful of every meal, every drink, and every exercise. It is extremely hard to take care of your body, but it is also hard to rack up doctor bills or buy new clothes by not taking care of your body. You will have to become more disciplined in your actions.

Be Disciplined

You will have to be disciplined to be successful. You must be disciplined to get your life to the next level. The discipline to work hard when nobody's watching. The discipline to go right when everyone else is going left. The discipline to say no when everybody around you is saying yes.

You also have to be discipline not to pull up to the local fast-food spot and grab your favorite treats. But there is a reward for the people who have the most discipline. Discipline equals freedom. And if you want to win your freedom, then you will have to have the discipline to add perseverance, endurance, and consistency to your life.

I knew that if I was going to be a successful father, husband, entrepreneur, and motivational speaker, I needed to be disciplined in my actions to start to take care of my body. So I became disciplined. I became disciplined with going to bed early or on time. I became disciplined in waking up earlier. I became disciplined in working out first thing in the morning. I became disciplined in working out even when I didn't want to. I also became disciplined enough to commit to living a cleaner lifestyle.

Commit To Living A Cleaner Lifestyle

Say what you want about Curtis "50 Cent" Jackson, but he is brilliant. The man has turned his life around from being shot nine times in the streets of New York to being a platinum-selling rap star. Once his rap career started to fade, 50 Cent became an actor, executive, and bonafide business mogul. 50 Cent has also written a few books in his spare time. In his book, *Hustle Harder Hustle Smarter,* 50 Cent talks about taking his life to the next level once he committed to living a cleaner lifestyle.

50 Cent states that it is not enough to work hard. You must commit to lifestyle choices that give you the energy, focus, and stamina to do the work. For 50 Cent, this meant abstaining from drugs and alcohol. 50 Cent later went on to say as you grow older, you will need to try to preserve your body proactively. He says the best way to do that is by eating right and working out.

Like 50 Cent, I chose to build a lifestyle that doesn't include drugs and alcohol. I've had some bad experiences with alcohol in my past that could have cost me everything I have now. I remember (sort of) drinking so much one night out that I decided to leave a party and walk home in the rain.

I left without telling my friends where I was going. I just left! Later that night, I blacked out on the side of the road. When my friends noticed that I was missing, they came looking for me. They found me as I was coming back to life on the side of the road, drenched from the rain and wet grass.

Nowadays, I'd rather drink ginger ale than liquor, and I've never really been into drugs. I don't judge the people who partake, but as you can probably tell, I can't function well when I'm under the influence. Who knows what could have happened to me if my friends didn't come looking for me when they did? And as a family man and an entrepreneur, my family and my business need my mind to be clear and able to focus on continuing to lead.

Eat Better

As I mentioned earlier, I love to eat. I probably have a go-to meal at all of the local fast-food chains near me. But at some point, I realized that I could no longer eat what I wanted whenever I wanted and look and feel the way I wanted. I had to figure out a new relationship with food. So I began to switch things up.

I began to no longer buy soft drinks, chips, cakes, and candy. I began to pay attention to things like carbs and processed foods. I began to read the back of labels before I would purchase items. I began to eat more fruits and vegetables. I began to drink more water. Most of all, I started to write down what foods I ate daily.

Each of these small changes led to a big difference on the scale. More importantly, these small changes led to big changes in my body. My body started to look good again. And when you look good, you feel good!

Work Out

Working out is hard work. But you know what they say about hard work. Hard work hurts, but it works. Working out will help energize and condition your body to push through the long days and nights you will endure while getting to the next level. Working out changes not only your body but also your mind, attitude, and mood. Working out can feel like a burden at first. But if you stay consistent, exercising will become a part of a better you.

While working out is paramount to your success because it will give you greater pride in your body and self-confidence, it does not have to be a complicated process. You can hire a fitness trainer or work out on your own. Studies have shown that simply working out 20 to 30 minutes 3-4 times a week will improve your overall health immensely. This can be achieved by simply walking, jogging, swimming, cycling, or yoga.

My workout consisted of each morning waking up at 6 am heading to the neighborhood trail, and walking while listening to motivational speeches. Doing this daily helped to get my body into shape and stimulate my mind by starting my day off with a heavy dose of positivity. This helped me both physically and mentally.

The trail is 1.77 miles. When I started walking the trail, I was only committed to going one time around. After a while, I increased my commitment to going at least twice. I started at the beginning like a tortoise, but now I'm like a cheetah out there! Nowadays, you can catch me rounding that trail three times. That's five miles.

My workouts are moved indoors to our home gym during the winter months. My indoor workouts consist of non-weight work like pushups, sit-ups, jumping rope, and resistance bands. My workouts are always a work in progress. But I am committed to putting the work in to make progress.

Chuck's Key #6:

Be Grateful and Thankful For It All

Be grateful and thankful for it all. I constantly tell myself to be grateful for everything, especially when I feel mad about something. And just as soon as you think you have it bad, someone always wishes they had your problems. Because truth be told, this is a cold world.

I'm so grateful and thankful for it all. Les Brown says one of the things that we know about life is that it is constantly changing. Sometimes you're up. Sometimes you're down. Sometimes you're happy. Sometimes you're sad. That's this thing called life.

This is true. There will be things that happen to you in your life that will catch you completely by surprise. Some things will be for your good. At the same time, others will bring you down to your knees. Life will not always give you a fair shake.

If nothing has happened to you yet, wait because your turn will surely come. Whenever I'm working on something big, something happens to the people closest to me. I have had my share of joy and pain, but I will remain thankful through it all.

Kenyatta's Car Accident

In 2018, my entrepreneurial career was finally taking off. I had gained enough momentum and closed enough deals to move out of my garage office into a nice-sized office. While finishing up a business meeting at my new office, I received a phone call from an unknown number. On the other end was a man's voice informing me that my wife, Kenyatta, was involved in a bad accident.

I raced out of the office and got to the scene of the accident as fast as I could. When I pulled up, I noticed two things. The first thing was how smashed up my wife's care was. The next thing I noticed was that the ambulance had not left for the hospital yet.

This caused me to panic, as I didn't know if she had survived the car crash. But as I walked to the ambulance, I could hear my wife's voice. She was beaten up pretty badly and would be down for a while. Her car was totaled. Her ankle was broken, and her teeth needed to be repaired. But she was alive. Nonetheless, I was grateful and thankful for it all.

Liberty's Illness

In 2019, my daughter Liberty developed some illness that temporarily caused her to lose feeling in her arms and legs. In a few days, she went from a healthy kid to being admitted to the hospital until further notice. I was shocked. I remember saying, "I can't believe this is happening to us! What is going on?"

As fate would have it, the very next second, I saw a young girl roll by us in a wheelchair with no legs. At that moment, it dawned on me that Liberty's sickness was most likely temporary while this young girl had permanent damage. I realized that soon Liberty would be back to normal while this young girl would be in her wheelchair, possibly for the rest of her life. I stopped complaining at that moment. As I said, be grateful and thankful for it all.

Though you may not focus on it, no matter how minor it is, there will always be something good about your life. Whether it's a roof over your head, food on the table, having good people around you, and so on, we should all pause to notice and appreciate the good things about our lives.

Mom's Fight

As a kid, I used to get sick all of the time. Anytime there was a seasonal change, I got sick. I'm talking about allergic reactions in the spring, asthma attacks in the summer, head colds in the fall, and catching the flu in the winter. My doctor's office was practically on speed dial.

However, I don't remember my parents being sick often, especially my mom, Cynthia. Maybe she was too busy caring for me, my sister, and my dad to ever get sick. But this all changed for me one summer when my mom had to cancel a vacation trip because she was feeling ill.

After months of doctor visit after doctor visits and test after test, my mom was diagnosed with cancer. The official diagnosis was multiple myeloma. We were told that even though multiple myeloma is treatable, it is incurable. My mom was now in for the fight of her life.

They say if you have a heartbeat, you will have heartache. And the cancer diagnosis broke my entire family's heart. We were devastated. The cancer diagnosis sucked. It was such a hard pill to swallow. My mom went from someone who rarely gets sick to now staring death in the face. This immediately changed the dynamics of my mom's life.

My mom always had a great spirit within her about enjoying life. But with the cancer diagnosis, she became even more grateful for each day she survived. Cancer made her more appreciative of the love and support that surrounded her. She understood that she didn't have to fight cancer alone. We would be right there fighting beside her.

My mom's cancer was a worthy opponent. It wreaked havoc on her body. It caused her to lose weight. It caused her to lose her hair. It caused her pain. It made her tired. It even made her unable to walk at times.

But my mom ain't never been "no punk." And every day, she showed up to fight. Some days were tougher than others. Some days it seemed like cancer was going to win. But she kept fighting. Eventually, my mom's fighting paid off when her cancer went into remission. Again be grateful and thankful for it all.

Gratitude

Life has a habit of being hard sometimes. Once you become an adult, you will go through things you never thought you'd go through. But that also means life can take you places you never thought you'd get to. Gratitude can greatly benefit us physically, mentally, emotionally, and socially. That is why you should be thankful for it all.

Challenge yourself to reduce the way you complain about things. A great way of practicing gratitude is to make it your habit to focus on the positive things in your life. Try to block out the things that aren't making you happy. Instead, create time daily to appreciate the things around you that make you happy. Happiness aids gratitude!

In my lifetime, I have been through countless tragedies. Some of them are harder than others, but each one hurts in its own little way. But again, that is life! Everybody has something going on.

Life isn't always great, but it's about how we react. So change how you respond to things and be grateful for it all. Be grateful for everything. Be grateful for every day that you wake up. Never hesitate to be thankful in any situation you find yourself in! Be grateful and thankful every day.

Chuck's Key #7:

Bless Somebody Else

We should all learn to serve by blessing somebody else. It's crazy to say this out loud, but I get more enjoyment from serving people than I do from cashing a big check. True story. I once went to a Chase bank to deposit a nice-sized check. In my mind, I thought the teller would acknowledge the significant amount written on the check.

To my surprise, she didn't say much of anything. She printed out my receipt and told me to have a nice day. I realized that day that having money in my bank account would not fulfill me. Don't get me wrong, I like to get to the money just like the next man, but to get your life to the next level, you must serve others.

My definition of serving others is to give your time, give your money, and give words of encouragement to the people in need around you. Don't ever get tired of helping others. Try your best to be a blessing to others. It's such a powerful feeling to bless someone because it's one of the only times you can feel fulfilled.

Generosity is doing something for somebody else while expecting nothing in return. Denzel Washington once said that the most selfish thing you can do in this world is to help somebody else. Why is it selfish? Because nothing is better than the gratification and good feelings you get from helping with your heart. Success is in the giving and not the taking. Generosity is like a gift that keeps on giving. This is the best part of generosity.

Everybody can be great because anybody can serve. As long as there are people in this world, there will be somebody you can help. We all have something to give to make the world a better place. There are so many ways of being of service to others.

For example, I serve others by mentoring young men in my local community. I call these young men my nephews. All my nephews know that I'm just a phone call away and am willing to serve at any moment. That's just how I am. I was put on this earth to uplift and empower people and make them feel good inside.

Why Not Give?

The main reason why people avoid helping and blessing others is that they think they don't have enough. Or they may need to be rich to some extent before blessing others. Many people in the world have been conditioned to have a scarcity mentality. This mindset is wrong.

Having a scarcity mindset will keep you from achieving your dreams. You need to operate with an abundance mindset. But understand that you don't have to be a millionaire before you can bless somebody else. You don't have to have much money at all. In fact, all that is required of you is to have the heart to serve others willingly.

Motivational speaker and fitness trainer DeWayne Montgomery, better known as Coach Pain, says that you can't come back once your life is over. So you better leave your mark while you can. Bless somebody. Lift somebody up when they're down. Be the strength for others when they're weak. And when you're at the lowest point in your life, they will lift you up.

What Are You Doing To Help The Person Next To You?

What are you doing to help the person next to you? There are countless ways to bless somebody else. Just pick one. If that doesn't work, create a new way to help. I have personally been involved in several ways. At my church, they say it is a blessing to be a blessing. So outside of mentoring young men in the community, my immediate family has established other ways we serve.

My wife once worked at Grady Memorial Hospital in Atlanta, Georgia. On her way home, she noticed that on a nearby street, there was a large population of homeless people. Riding past this homeless population sparked something inside of her. She wanted to be a blessing to the homeless community. After brainstorming together, we came up with a plan to make it our mission to create care packets for those families in need. Each packet contained items like toothbrushes, toothpaste, deodorant, socks, sanitation items, water, fruit, etc.

Each time we would deliver those care packets, we would do it as a family. We all wanted to be a part of helping others in need. It was something about the faces of the people we were serving when they realized what they were receiving. Even though we were the ones who were serving others, we felt as if we were the ones who were rewarded.

Blessing somebody else is contagious. Once you start, it will be hard to stop. Every time you bless somebody else, it has the potential to create a ripple effect that could have limitless potential. Quite often, you can find me or my wife inspired enough to pay for other families' groceries at the local food mart. We have even been known to pay for the person's goods in line behind us at the store or in the drive-through. It's all spontaneous. We serve only from the heart.

Frances Harbin Brown Foundation

My family and I were inspired to give back to our community a few years ago. We were not sure what we could do to help. Eventually, we decided to honor my grandmother's legacy by providing college-bound students from our community with scholarships. We decided to create a foundation. We named the foundation the Frances Harbin Brown Foundation (FHB) after my late grandmother.

Starting a foundation from the ground up was a challenging task. No one in my family had ever created a foundation like the one we wanted to create. However, after initially struggling to raise capital for the non-profit organization, we launched the scholarship fund in 2016 with the help of friends and family.

The FHB Foundation has grown in its six years of existence. Since 2016, we have been able to provide scholarships to students attending universities like the University of Louisville, Indiana University, Western Kentucky University, Murray State University, and Georgia State University.

Our scholarship recipients are each performing well and are expected to graduate on time. We hope each student will graduate and continue uplifting our community positively.

In addition to our involvement with the Frances Harbin Brown Foundation, my family and I have traveled across the country doing mission work. We have been to countries like Jamaica and South Africa to provide various resources, including medical assistance and personal inspiration, to people in need.

When doing mission work, you truly understand how impactful blessing someone else can be. People who do not have much are genuinely touched when you are able to gift them even with the smallest amount of goods. Mission work has inspired me never to stop blessing someone else. How can you and your family bless someone else?

Conclusion

Getting to the next level in your life will take time. There is nothing more powerful than a changed mind. And once you have your mind made up to get to the next level, nothing will stop you. However, your transformation will take time.

This journey will test you mentally, physically, and spiritually. Know that you already have everything inside of you. However, you must activate your skills so that they can help take your life to new heights.

Remember that God has your back. Decide that despite all the obstacles that may come your way, you will not quit. Implement my seven keys as a new life mindset. Then you will begin to level up no matter what! NO MATTER WHAT!

About the Author

Chuck Collins is a native of Louisville, Kentucky. He is an Atlanta businessman, author, and mentor currently residing in Georgia. Chuck is a husband, father, visionary, leader, go-getter, and has a special talent for entrepreneurship. Chuck is the CEO of many businesses but feels that motivational speaking is his truest gift. When Chuck speaks, he lets the world witness his testimony and truth.

Regardless of the industry, Chuck has become a favorite speaker for his clients. His blend of comedy and motivation in his keynotes leaves the audience wanting more. Chuck lives in Georgia with his wife and daughter. When he is not traveling around the country speaking, Chuck can be found mentoring others or serving his community.

For media requests or to book as a speaker, please email chuck@chuckcollinsbrand.com. Visit his website at www.chuckcollinsbrand.com.

Level Up No Matter What!
Reflections Section

In this section, reflect on what points you connected with and will work on to take your life to new heights. It is time to Level Up No Matter What!

_____

_____

_____

_____

_____

_____

_____

_____

_____

_____

_____

_____

_____

_____

_____

_____

_____

_____

_____

_____

_____

_____

_____

_____

_____

_____

_____

_____

_____

_____

_____

_____

_____

_____

_____

_____

_____

_____

_____

_____

_____

_____

_____

_____

_____

_____

_____

_____

_____

_____

_____

_____

_____

_____

_____

_____

_____

_____

_____

_____

_____

_____

_____

_____

_____

_____

_____

_____

_____

_____

_____

_____

_____

_____

_____

_____

_____

_____

_____

_____

_____

_____

_____

_____

_____

_____

_____

_____

_____

_____

_____

_____

_____

_____

_____

_____

_____

_____

_____

_____

_____

_____

_____

_____

_____

_____

_____

_____

_____

_____

_____

_____

_____

_____

_____

_____

_____

_____

_____

_____

Chuck Collins

_____

_____

_____

_____

_____

_____

_____

_____

_____

_____

_____

_____

_____

_____

_____

_____

_____

_____

_____

_____

_____

_____

_____

_____

_____

_____

_____

_____

_____

_____

_____

_____

_____

_____

_____

_____

_____

_____

_____

_____

_____

_____

_____

_____

_____

_____

_____

_____

_____

_____

_____

_____

_____

_____

_____

_____

_____

_____